EXPLORER TRAVEL

WITHDRAWN

Anna Claybourne

Chicago, Illinois

Edited by Adam Miller, Laura Knowles, and Claire Throp
Designed by Steve Mead
Original illustrations © Capstone Global Library Ltd 2014
Illustrated by H L Studios
Picture research by Tracy Cummins
Production by Victoria Fitzgerald
Originated by Capstone Global Library Ltd
Printed in China by China Translation and Printing Services

17 16 15 14 13
10 9 8 7 6 5 4 3 2 1

Library of Congress Cataloging-in-Publication Data
Claybourne, Anna.
  Caves / Anna Claybourne.
    p. cm.—(Explorer travel guides)
  Includes bibliographical references and index.
  ISBN 978-1-4109-5428-2 (hb)—ISBN 978-1-4109-5435-0 (pb) 1. Caves—Juvenile literature. I. Title.
  GB601.2.C53 2013
  796.52'5—dc23   2012042340

Acknowledgments

The author and publisher are grateful to the following for permission to reproduce copyright material: Alamy p. 20 (© Interfoto); AP Photo p. 16 (Susan Montoya Bryan); Caveslime.org p. 35 (© Kenneth Ingham); Corbis pp. 27 (© Rafael Duran/Reuters), 33 (© Imaginechina), 39 (© Jean-Daniel Sudres/Hemis); Getty Images pp. 6 (National Geographic/Jim Richardson), 8 (Carsten Peter/Speleoresearch & Films/National Geographic), 9 (Carsten Peter/National Geographic), 15 (Jonathan S. Blair/National Geographic), 19 (Henrik Sorensen); Library of Congress, Prints and Photographs Division p. 7; Martyn Farr pp. 5 middle, 28 (© Martyn Farr); National Geographic Stock pp. 14 (Amy Toensing), 21 (Bill Hatcher), 24, 34 (Stephen Alvarez); Photo Researchers, Inc. p. 31 (Tom McHugh); Shutterstock pp. 5 bottom, 32 (© Dziewul), 5 top, 13 (© Jeff Schultes), 18 (© salajean), 22 (© Vitalii Nesterchuk), 30 (© Bryan Brazil); Superstock pp. 4 (© Photononstop), 11 (© Rapsodia), 25 (© Prisma), 37 (© Science Faction).

Design elements: Shutterstock (© MountainHardcore), (© Nik Merkulov), (© vovan), (© SmileStudio), (© Petrov Stanislav Eduardovich), (© Nataliia Natykach), (© Phecsone).

Cover photograph of two cave explorers in Mulu National Park reproduced with permission of Superstock (© Robbie Shone/Aurora Open).

We would like to thank Daniel Block for his invaluable help in the preparation of this book.

Every effort has been made to contact copyright holders of any material reproduced in this book. Any omissions will be rectified in subsequent printings if notice is given to the publisher.

All the Internet addresses (URLs) given in this book were valid at the time of going to press. However, due to the dynamic nature of the Internet, some addresses may have changed, or sites may have changed or ceased to exist since publication. While the author and publisher regret any inconvenience this may cause readers, no responsibility for any such changes can be accepted by either the author or the publisher.

CONTENTS

Some words are shown in bold, **like this**. You can find out what they mean by looking in the glossary.

Don't forget
These boxes will give you handy tips and remind you what to take on your caving adventures.

Amazing facts
Check out these boxes for amazing cave facts and figures.

Who's who
Find out more about cave experts and explorers of the past.

Conservation
Learn about conservation issues relating to caves.

DESTINATION: AN UNDERGROUND WORLD

Deep down under the ground, there lies a hidden world. There are dark, dripping passageways, huge cave chambers, narrow tunnels, and underground rivers, lakes, and waterfalls. There are giant crystals, alien-looking rock shapes, and bizarre cave creatures creeping through the gloom. Caves are found all over the world, creating a secret maze that most of us never think about. There could be an unknown cave system under your feet right now, waiting to be discovered.

This high-ceilinged, echoing cave chamber is in a cave system in Gard, in southern France.

Let's explore!

Going underground to explore caves is incredibly exciting. They are dark, damp, strange, beautiful, and among the most remote and undiscovered parts of our planet. Cave explorers are always finding amazing new underground chambers, tunnels, and rock formations that no one has ever seen before.

What's inside?

Besides the caves and rocks themselves, explorers find all sorts of fascinating things inside cave systems. You might stumble across important fossils or crumbling human skeletons, precious minerals, prehistoric tools and pottery, mysterious ancient art and writings, or maybe a new **species** of bat, toad, or spider.

Amazing facts

The world's longest cave, Mammoth Cave in central Kentucky, has over 390 miles (628 kilometers) of passageways discovered so far, with more still to explore...

Turn the page...

See page 12 to read about stalactites and stalagmites—and page 35 for snottites!

Meet real-life cave explorers on pages 16 and 28.

Turn to page 32 to find out about what living in a cave is like.

DISCOVERING CAVES

Humans have always known about caves, as prehistoric peoples used them for shelter (see page 30). But even after thousands of years of exploring them, we still have not discovered them all.

Caves in the ancient world

Some ancient peoples thought caves had magical or mystical properties. The ancient Greeks believed you could discover wisdom from the gods by going underground. The famous Greek playwright Euripides was said to spend most of his time in a gloomy cave facing the sea on the island of Salamis, thinking to himself and writing his tragic plays.

Fingal's Cave, an unusual and awe-inspiring sea cave in Scotland, was one of the first caves to become a famous tourist attraction.

Early cave explorers

Modern cave exploration really took off in the 1700s, when people began looking for caves, investigating them, and writing about them. In 1772, scientist Joseph Banks famously "discovered" and named Fingal's Cave (see the photo on page 6), a stunning sea cave on the isle of Staffa in Scotland. Locals had known about it for centuries and called it the Cave of Melody, because of the strange, musical sounds it makes as crashing waves echo around the walls. But Banks's description made it famous and inspired thousands of people to visit it. He wrote: "Compared to this what are the cathedrals and palaces built by men! Mere models or playthings..."

? Who's who

Stephen Bishop was an African American slave who became a great cave expert and guide. His owner, Franklin Gorin, bought Mammoth Cave in Kentucky in 1838, and he gave Bishop the job of exploring it. Bishop discovered large parts of the cave, made maps of it, and named many parts of it, such as the "Snowball Room" and "Little Bat Avenue." Bishop was eventually freed from slavery in 1856.

Bigger and bigger

Early explorers had to brave unknown caves with little more than an oil lantern. Today, thanks to modern inventions such as electric head flashlights and **scuba** gear, we can explore further and deeper.

As cave explorers find new passageways, the known length of a cave grows. For example, explorers first started mapping Ox Bel Ha, a water-filled cave system in Mexico, in the 1990s, and it soon became the world's longest known underwater cave. In 2007, another Mexican system, Sac Actun, stole the title, reaching 134 miles (215 kilometers) in length. In 2011, Ox Bel Ha grabbed it back, when divers found a connection to another system that made it 135 miles (216 kilometers) long. Ox Bel Ha now measures over 144 miles (230 kilometers), but the two systems keep competing for the record.

This cave explorer has lots of hi-tech cave mapping and monitoring gear, as well as a cooling suit to battle the high temperatures deep underground.

This geologist (Earth scientist) is studying a map showing the underground faults and cracks of a cave system in Vietnam.

Cave maps

Mapping caves is tricky, since they are 3D systems. Tunnels can go up or down as well as along, and they can pass over and under each other. To make a detailed map, cave explorers use tapes to measure passageways and waterproof paper to sketch them. They enter their results into special cave-mapping software, which creates a 3D map.

Amazing facts

The deepest cave discovered so far is Krubera-Voronja Cave in Georgia, a small country between Russia and Turkey. At its lowest point, it is a deep, dark 7,189 feet (2,191 meters) below ground level.

CAVE SCIENCE

Most caves started off as solid rock and have formed gradually over thousands of years, thanks to the action of water. As rain falls through the air and into the soil, it soaks up a small amount of carbon dioxide, making a weak acid. This acid can slowly dissolve some types of rock, especially **limestone** and similar rocks such as **dolomite** and **marble**. **Gypsum**, a different type of rock, is also often dissolved to form caves.

Dripping and draining

Caves form when this slightly acidic rainwater soaks into cracks in these types of rock. As it drips and drains through the cracks, it slowly dissolves the rock, and the cracks get wider and deeper. Over time, this process hollows out whole cave systems. Areas made up of these dissolvable rocks are known as **karst** landscapes and usually have lots of caves.

Who's who

Jovan Cvijić (1865–1927) was a Serbian scientist who studied the way water forms caves. He explored and wrote about caves in an area of Europe known as Kras, Carsa, or Karst. Limestone landscapes all over the world are now known as "karst" landscapes, thanks to his work.

Other caves

Caves can form in other ways, too:

- Rock can be eaten away by acid from underground **bacteria**.
- Lava from a volcano can form tube-shaped tunnels as it cools and hardens.
- Ocean waves, carrying sand and pebbles, can wear away rocks at the coast to form sea caves.
- Wind that blasts sand at rock faces, usually in deserts, can hollow out cliff caves.

Amazing facts

When does a crack become a cave? Spaces underground are described as caves once they are big enough for humans to explore.

This is a typical water-filled cavern inside a karst limestone cave, in the Grotte de la Cabane Cave in France.

Speleothems

In karst or limestone caves, the cave walls, floors, and ceilings are spiky, lumpy, and rough, thanks to all the strange rock formations, or **speleothems**, that grow there. Speleothems form as cave water leaves some of the rock dissolved in it behind, building up new rocky shapes. The way the rock is deposited can create beautiful bands of different colors, smooth or rippling textures, and amazingly delicate structures.

Sticking up and hanging down

The most famous speleothems are **stalactites** and **stalagmites**. Stalactites are pointy spikes that hang down from cave ceilings. They grow as water drips from a crack in the roof, leaving a little bit of stone behind with each drip. Then, as the water drips onto the ground, more rock builds up to make an upward-pointing stalagmite. After thousands of years, a stalactite and stalagmite may meet in the middle, forming a pillar or column.

Rock formations inside a karst cave

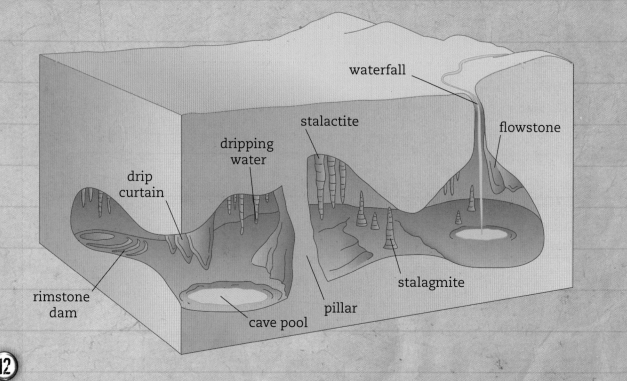

waterfall

stalactite

flowstone

dripping water

drip curtain

stalagmite

rimstone dam

cave pool

pillar

Sheets and curtains

If water flows over a flat surface, such as down a cave wall, it can build up a smooth, pale sheet of stone called a **flowstone**. Sometimes the water flows in ripples, creating a rumpled-looking stone **drip curtain**. Cave pools can also deposit rock around their edges, making a little wall or **rimstone dam**. Speleothems can also include needles, spirals, spheres, hollow straws, cones, flowers, and shapes that look like huge iced cakes.

Some cave chambers are so stuffed with speleothems that you cannot see the original walls or ceiling at all!

Don't forget

Caves are mainly made by water, and so they are often full of water—which is one of the biggest dangers for explorers. If you cannot swim, you should learn to do so before starting your cave adventure!

Take your pick!

The study of caves is called **speleology**. If you would like to spend your life studying things in caves, there are plenty of careers to choose from—as long as you do not mind a few long words!

- Biospeleologists study living things found in caves, from bats to underwater cave creatures and fungi.
- Speleopaleontologists search for and study fossils found in caves, to find out about plants and animals of the past.
- Speleoarchaeologists look at things left behind in caves by people from the past, showing how caves were used.
- A hydrogeologist studies underground water and how it moves.
- Karst geomorphologists study the formation of caves and other karst landforms.

These two scientists are carefully excavating ancient animal bones from Dead End Den Cave in Tasmania, Australia.

Out and about

Most cave scientists go into caves regularly to do **fieldwork**. For example, a biospeleologist might count bats leaving a cave at night, search for unknown species, or collect cave animals' droppings to find out about their diet. So, just like other cave explorers, speleologists have to know how to use caving equipment and stay safe in a cave.

In the lab

To study the things they find in more detail, scientists may need to take them back to a **laboratory**, where they can use microscopes or chemical reactions to find out more about them. They have to label everything and pack it up carefully to transport it to the surface.

Conservation

Scientists working in caves may have to dig up fossils or artifacts, collect samples of living things, or take away pieces of speleothems—behavior that is not normally allowed in caves! They have to arrange special scientific permission first and try to have as little impact on the cave as possible.

This scientist is cleaning and sorting out a set of bones discovered in a lava tube cave in Maui, Hawaii.

INTERVIEW WITH A CAVE SCIENTIST

← Professor Penny Boston is a mixture of speleologist, microbiologist, and astrobiologist! She studies tiny creatures such as bacteria living in extreme habitats, including caves. She also studies other planets and moons, to look for signs of life there.

Q: What made you interested in caves?
A: At first, I studied **microorganisms** (tiny living things) in other environments, and I became interested in the subsurface of Mars as a place where life might exist. That made me start searching for life under Earth's surface, by going into caves and mines.

Q: How do you prepare for a caving trip?
A: It depends on the cave. For a relatively shallow type of cave, like a volcanic lava tube, we dress in clothes to suit the temperature, take cave helmets and lights, and pack science gear ready for any tests we want to do or samples we want to take. For a very deep cave, we would get our vertical gear ready—ropes for going up and down cliffs in caves.

Q: What's the most exciting thing you've discovered?

A: Finding out how underground microorganisms get their energy from minerals, like iron and sulfur, and live together in groups with other, different types of microorganisms. Many of them are also super-tiny. They are called nanobacteria because of this small size.

Q: What's the most amazing cave you've visited?

A: There are so many, but I think the Cave of the Crystals in Mexico is one. It's extremely hot there, so we have to wear special suits with ice in them to keep us cool enough to work. Also Lechuguilla Cave in New Mexico— it has gigantic cathedral-sized rooms, rock mazes that we have to crawl through, pink and peach-colored stalagmites and stalactites, and passages covered in gypsum crystals that look like sparkly glitter.

Q: Do you ever get scared, or have you had any frightening moments?

A: Oh yes! One of the caves that we work in, Cueva de Villa Luz ("Cave of the Lighted House") in Tabasco, Mexico, has a lot of very poisonous gases in it. One time I was crawling along a very small passage between different parts of the cave, and my oxygen monitor showed that the oxygen level was dropping fast. I had to back out quickly before I became unconscious from lack of oxygen.

Q: Tell us about your work on life on other planets

A: We're studying images and other data from our Moon, from planets like Mars, and from moons around other planets, too, to look for evidence of caves where living things could exist.

Q: Do you think humans will end up living on other planets? If so, could they live in caves?

A: Maybe! I've been working on the idea of people living in lava tube caves on the Moon and Mars.

PREPARE FOR YOUR TRIP

Going caving is a thrilling adventure, but it can be dangerous if you are not properly prepared. Follow these rules to make sure you will see the light of day again!

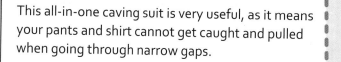

This all-in-one caving suit is very useful, as it means your pants and shirt cannot get caught and pulled when going through narrow gaps.

Conservation

It is important to keep caves in their natural, unspoiled condition. So remember...

- Take all your litter out with you.

- Don't break off, damage, or remove any part of the cave.

- Don't disturb wildlife.

- No fires, smoking, or going to the bathroom!

Caving common sense

Never go caving by yourself, and don't start exploring a cave on a whim—it is easy to get lost. Before a caving trip, plan where you are going and check the weather forecast. If there is going to be heavy rain, don't go, because caves can flood quickly, trapping you inside. Always leave details of your trip, and when you expect to come back, with someone else. If you don't return, that person can alert others.

What to wear

Caving is a lot like hiking and climbing, but in dark, slippery, wet, cold conditions. You need modern hiking boots with a good grip, even in wet conditions. Wear wool socks and layers of warm clothes, but nothing too bulky. Avoid flaps and pockets that could get caught on rocks. Kneepads are useful for crawling, and gloves with a good grip can protect your hands from sharp rocks.

Cavers need at least two flashlights, ideally three—in case one gets dropped or wet or runs out of batteries.

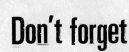 # Don't forget

Your essential caving kit should include:

helmet
head flashlight
map and compass
two spare flashlights
spare batteries and bulbs
matches and candles
food and water
dry spare clothes
whistle
penknife
jar with lid (to use as a toilet!)
first aid kit
survival blanket.

WHO'S GOING WITH YOU?

If you could take anyone in the world, past or present, on your underground adventure, who would it be? These top cave experts would be a good place to start...

Expedition member:
Edouard Martel
(1859–1938)

Martel is known as the "father of modern speleology" (or cave science). He explored, mapped, sketched, and studied thousands of caves and led the way in making caving a popular sport.

Expert knowledge:
Vast experience of all types of caves

Expedition member: Norbert Casteret (1897–1987)

Casteret was a famous, brilliant, and swashbuckling caver who discovered many new caves, as well as cave art, ancient human remains, and prehistoric artifacts. He wrote many books about his adventures, which still inspire cavers.

Potential job: Caving skills, courage, and knowledge of ancient artifacts

Expedition member: Hazel Barton

A professor of biology and expert on bacteria found in caves, Barton (on the right) has years of caving experience and a great understanding of cave creatures and ecosystems.

Potential job: Vertical caving skills (see page 25), cave life scientist, team medic

Expedition member: Sheck Exley (1949-1994)

One of the most admired cave divers of all time, Exley pioneered the sport of **cave diving** and developed many new safety and rescue techniques.

Potential job: Cave diving and rescue

Don't forget

To be as safe as possible, there should be a minimum of three people on your caving team, including at least one experienced caver.

DOWN WE GO!

You have your team, your equipment, and your lunchbox—you are finally ready to go underground! As you descend into the dank and dark depths, try to remember these handy caving tips...

Cavers sometimes call a narrow gap like this a squeeze, a pinch, or a "flattener."

Bump!

You are wearing a helmet for a reason. Low ceilings, spikes that stick out, and even falling rocks mean cavers are constantly at risk of a bump on the head. You could also trip on the uneven cave floor or on a pile of loose rubble. Always go slowly, step carefully, and remember to be aware of what is near your head.

Don't get stuck!

Squeezing through tiny gaps is one of the scariest parts of caving, and even experienced cavers have been known to get stuck. Don't try to get through a gap unless you are sure you will fit!

I can't see!

Caves aren't just dark—they are completely pitch-black. Without your flashlight, you will be totally blind, so hang onto it. Even with a flashlight, it is quite gloomy, so stay on the lookout for dangers.

Slipping and sliding

Cave pools, waterfalls, and slimy wet surfaces can make getting around very slippery, so be careful. It is especially important not to fall into the water, as you could be swept away or get dangerously cold.

Don't forget

When you go into a cave, you need to find your way out! You should not damage or mark cave systems or leave anything behind in them. So, the best ways to keep track of your route are with small piles of stones or with temporary pieces of sticky tape that you collect on your way out.

Vertical cavers tackle Mystery Falls, a deep cave pit containing a waterfall in Tennessee.

Extraordinary caving

If normal caving is not exciting enough, you could try these extra-challenging cave adventures. For some, you will need special equipment—and nerves of steel!

Glacier caves

Glaciers are huge flows of ice found on high mountains or around the poles. Caves sometimes form inside them as water runs into cracks and wears away hollows. **Glacier caves** are stunning, with sparkling blue ice everywhere you look. However, they can be dangerous, because they can melt or collapse quickly. You will need spiky **crampons** on your boots to give you a good grip.

Ice caves

Ice caves are normal rock caves, but with ice inside. They are often found in mountain and polar areas, where it is very cold. As water drips into an ice cave, it freezes, building breathtaking speleothems made of ice instead of rock.

Amazing facts

Cave diving is one of the world's most dangerous sports. Quite a few explorers have died doing it.

Cave climbing or "vertical caving"

By combining caving with rock climbing, you can climb up and **abseil** down cliffs, caverns, waterfalls, and chimneys inside cave systems. You need special gear such as climbing ropes and harnesses. Cave climbing can damage caves, so vertical cavers must be careful to avoid breaking or marking the rocks.

Cave diving

The ultimate caving challenge, "cave diving" means exploring completely water-filled cave chambers and tunnels using scuba diving gear. You also need water-safe flashlights and back-up emergency equipment, so cave divers have to carry a lot with them.

This cave diver has been photographed underwater in Chandelier Cave on the Pacific island of Palau.

Don't panic!

Getting lost, injured, or stuck in a cave can be very scary, but don't panic! Follow these survival tips and you should be OK. Here is what to do if...

... you get totally lost.

Sit down together, stay calm, keep warm and dry, and ration your food and flashlight batteries. Rescuers should come looking for you, so call or whistle for help regularly. Three loud blasts on your whistle means "HELP!"

... someone gets hurt and can't move.

Send one or more cavers to get help, while others stay with the injured person. Use first aid to treat wounds, keep the person warm, and give him or her something to drink.

... you get stuck in a tight space.

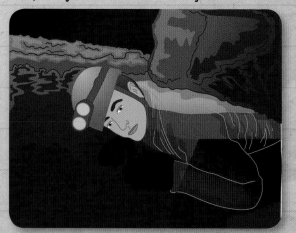

Stay calm and breathe slowly. Breathing out is the best way to make yourself as small as possible to try to get free. Another caver should then be able to push or pull you out.

... you get cut off by floodwater.

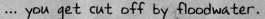

Trying to swim out is too risky. Stay where you are and wait for help.

... you're left without a light source.

... you get bitten by a bat or another animal.

Everyone should sit down and hold onto each other, so no one gets lost. Then wait to be rescued.

Animals can sometimes carry diseases such as rabies, which is found in some bats. It is very rare, but it needs to be treated quickly. So if an animal bites you, see a doctor as soon as possible and explain what happened.

Hypothermia

One of the deadliest dangers while caving is **hypothermia**, or getting too cold. The signs include feeling cold, shivering, then becoming slow and confused. If this happens to anyone, everyone should leave the cave. Wrap cold people up and cuddle or rub them, to warm them up.

These cavers are waiting for rescuers to come and search for the rest of their team, who have been cut off by water inside the cave.

INTERVIEW WITH A CAVE EXPLORER

← Martyn Farr is a world-renowned caver, cave diver, photographer, author, and teacher. He has spent more than 50 years exploring caves and discovering many new systems and passageways.

Q: What's a typical day like when you're exploring?

A: You spend a lot of time preparing your equipment, checking it, and making a plan. By the time you get to the cave, you feel tense and nervous, especially on cave dives. But once you take the plunge, the fear disappears, and focus takes over. You concentrate 100 percent on what you have to do: get as far as possible, and return safely.

Q: What's the hardest part of cave diving, and what's the best?

A: Oh, by far the best is when you reach a place where no one has ever been before, and you're exploring somewhere totally new. It's a massive buzz! The hardest part is after that, when you have to get back. If you don't make it out alive, what you've discovered won't mean anything.

Q: What's the most important piece of equipment?

A: I always tell my students that *all* their equipment matters—it's like a chain: if any link in the chain breaks, you're in trouble. But if your scuba or lighting gear fails, it's immediately a life-or-death situation.

Q: Where's your favorite cave in the world?

A I'd have to say a cave in South Wales called Dan-yr-Ogof. Part of it is open to the public, and that part is amazing enough. But beyond that, there are lakes, underwater tunnels, rock formations, and a very narrow passage called the Long Crawl. Ancient human bones have been found there, too.

Q: What do you take to eat and drink in a cave?

A: On a cave dive, you take water packs that you drink through a straw, but no food; you just keep dives to a maximum of 4–6 hours. When dry caving, you can take all kinds of food. High-energy chocolate and raisins are useful, but best of all is a nice sandwich! It sounds silly, but everyday food helps to keep your spirits up and makes you feel ready for anything.

Q: Who would you name as the greatest caver ever?

A: The French cave explorer Norbert Casteret (see page 20), who I was lucky enough to meet in the 1970s. He was one of the earliest pioneers of the sport and incredibly brave—he would just dive into a cave pool and hold his breath until he surfaced somewhere else. This was in the 1920s, before scuba gear was invented. He took matches and candles in a dry container and lit them at the other end to see where he was!

Q: Why are caves so fascinating and important?

A: Caves are my passion and I've never gotten tired of them, because there's always something new. We know more about the surface of the Moon and the deep seabed than we do about what's under the ground. And there are so many different things to find there—new species of wildlife, fossils, ancient rock art. Caves have so many amazing secrets.

CAVE-DWELLERS

Caves were among the first human homes. They provide a natural shelter from the weather and protection from wild animals. We have discovered many caves around the world that people lived in long ago. Some contain ancient tools, skeletons, and other clues to life in the past.

Earliest peoples

The amazing Azykh Cave in Azerbaijan has been home to many different peoples over time, including some of the earliest of all. A **Neanderthal** woman's jawbone found there is over 300,000 years old, and ancient stone tools in the cave date from around a million years ago.

These homes, built into caves under overhanging cliffs, are in Colorado. They were built by the Anasazi people around the year 1200.

Human bones

In 1888, a cave in France, the Raymonden Shelter, was excavated. In addition to reindeer bones and lots of tools, it contained a whole Cro-Magnon male skeleton, buried about 12,000 years ago. Cro-Magnons were early modern humans. Caves often contain interesting bones that can tell us a lot about ancient peoples.

Amazing facts

Cartoons often show "cavemen" as simple early humans who say "Ug!" and carry a club to bash enemies on the head. In fact, many prehistoric cave-dwellers, like the Neanderthals and later the Cro-Magnons, were fairly advanced. They used complex language, made tools, cooked their food, and created artwork.

Paint and jewels

Exciting finds in Blombos Cave in South Africa show that people living there 80,000 to 100,000 years ago liked making art and jewelry. Archaeologists have found pieces of **ocher** clay decorated with patterns, beads made from painted shells, and tools for mixing up paints.

This is a recreation of what a Neanderthal cave-dweller from 100,000 years ago might have looked like. Neanderthals were related to humans, but they were a separate species.

Cool, green, and natural

Millions of people still live in cave houses in China, Spain, France, Turkey, and many other countries. Some are ancient caves that are still in use. Others are modern homes with electricity and running water, built into or onto an existing cave. So, what is living in a cave really like?

People who live in caves usually love their homes! A cave house is fairly cheap to build, since most of it is there already. It is eco-friendly, because it does not use up lots of materials or need many repairs. It does not take up valuable land (unless you want a yard, too). Cave houses are popular with people who want a unique home and like feeling close to nature.

Some of these cave houses in Cappadocia, in Turkey, are still used as homes today.

An elementary school class meets inside a large cave in Shuitang, China.

On the down side...

Cave houses can be damp, and some cave-dwellers have to pump moisture out of the air so that it does not collect inside. However, this can provide a handy water supply. Low, uneven ceilings mean you need to be careful about bumping your head!

More uses for caves

If you would like to spend a night in a cave, there are several cave hotels that you can go and stay in. Caves can also be used for other things—for example, one cave in China is used as a school classroom, and the Postojna Cave in Slovenia is a well-known concert venue.

Amazing facts

Caves actually make comfy homes because the thick stone stores up heat, helping them to stay warmer in winter and cooler in summer.

Cave creatures

Caves are home to all kinds of living things, and scientists divide these creatures into three main types:

- **Trogloxenes**, meaning "cave visitors": These animals use caves to take shelter or sleep in, but they also go outside—for example, to find food. Cave bats and moths are trogloxenes.

- **Troglophiles**, meaning "cave-lovers": These animals prefer caves, but can live outside them. Examples include some frogs, worms, and beetles.

- **Troglobites**, meaning "cave-livers": They spend their whole lives inside caves and cannot live outside. Because caves are dark, many of these animals are blind or almost blind. They include cave fish and shrimp and the Texas blind salamander.

Amazing facts

Bracken Cave in Texas is home to around 20 million Mexican free-tailed bats.

This cave crayfish is a typical troglobite, with its pale coloring and lack of eyesight.

Disgusting-looking, slimy snottites dangle from a cave roof.

Creature features

Troglobites can look quite strange. They are usually ghostly pale—there is no point having colors if there is no light! Many are blind and have no eyes, because they do not need them. Instead, they often have very good hearing or use their sense of touch to find food.

Life without light

Outside caves, plants make food for animals, using sunlight to grow. Caves are dark, which means that plants cannot grow there—they only live near cave entrances. But there are tiny single-celled bacteria in caves that provide food for animals. Instead of light, they get energy from cave rocks, minerals, or gases.

 ## Amazing facts

Instead of stalactites, some caves have **snottites**! Snottites are strings of wet, dripping slime hanging down from the ceiling, made of colonies of cave bacteria. Don't touch them, because they can drip acid that could burn you.

MUST-SEE CAVES

These are some of the most exciting caves to see around the world. They are not all open to the public, though, so you might need special permission to get in.

Cave of the Crystals, Naica, Mexico

This swelteringly hot, 1,000-foot- (300-meter-) deep cave is filled with stunning white crystals that are up to 36 feet (11 meters) long.

Mammoth Cave, Kentucky, United States

Mammoth Cave is an underground labyrinth and is the longest known cave system on Earth.

Sarawak Chamber, Borneo, Malaysia

This vast underground cavern is thought to be the world's biggest cave chamber.

Cave of the Swallows, San Luis Potosi, Mexico

This huge cave is 1,083 feet (330 meters) deep. It is rich in wildlife and is very popular with cave climbers.

Glowworm Cave, Waitomo, New Zealand

You can take a boat ride through this cave system to view its ceiling alight with glowworms.

Eisriesenwelt, Salzburg, Austria

Meaning "world of the ice giants," the world's biggest ice cave is open to visitors in the summer.

Amazing facts

In Luray Caverns, Virginia, the stalactites have been made into the world's biggest musical instrument, called the Stalacpipe Organ.

In many famous caves, you can go on a special guided tour, like these tourists taking a boat trip through Waigeo Caves in Indonesia.

Gaping Gill, England
Twice a year, caving groups set up a platform so visitors can be lowered down into this 330-foot- (100-meter-) deep cave shaft to look around.

Cueva del Fantasma (Cave of the Ghost), Guayana, Venezuela
This enormous cavern in the side of a cliff is worth visiting for its wildlife, waterfall, and breathtaking size.

Ellison's Cave, Georgia, United States
This very large and deep cave is not for tourists—only experienced cavers should explore it. It includes Fantastic Pit, a breathtaking vertical shaft that is 586 feet (180 meters) tall.

Azykh Cave, Tujh, Azerbaijan
A series of high-roofed chambers, home to a million years of history and prehistory, can be found in Azykh Cave.

Cave art

For art and history lovers, the caves listed here contain some of the world's most amazing ancient cave paintings and other rock art. Besides being beautiful, they can reveal things like how people hunted and what prehistoric animals looked like.

Lascaux, Dordogne, France

The famous cave paintings at Lascaux, in France, are about 20,000 years old and include bulls, horses, stags, other animals, human figures, and mysterious symbols.

Bhimbetka, Madhya Pradesh, India

This series of rock shelters contains hundreds of works of art created over thousands of years. They show many activities such as people getting dressed up, dancing, fighting, riding, and collecting food, and animals including crocodiles, elephants, tigers, lions, and dogs.

Cueva de las Manos (Cave of the Hands), Santa Cruz, Argentina

This cave system is most famous for its 10,000-year-old hand paintings, made by spraying paint around a hand to make a stencil-like mark on the wall.

Drakensberg Mountains, Southern Africa

In the hundreds of caves and rock shelters found throughout these mountains are thousands of paintings of animals, hunts, and ceremonies created by the San people around 20,000 years ago.

Amazing facts

The caves at Lascaux were discovered by four teenage boys in 1940, after their dog disappeared down a hole and they followed it.

Chauvet Cave, France

Chauvet Cave, only discovered in 1994, contains some of the oldest known cave paintings, dating from over 30,000 years ago. They include lions, bears, bison, and horses.

These animal pictures and writing-like symbols can be seen painted on the cave walls at Lascaux.

Don't forget

Some of these sites are closed to the public, and at others, you may not be able to take photos, because the flash can make the artwork fade over time.

CAVES OF THE WORLD

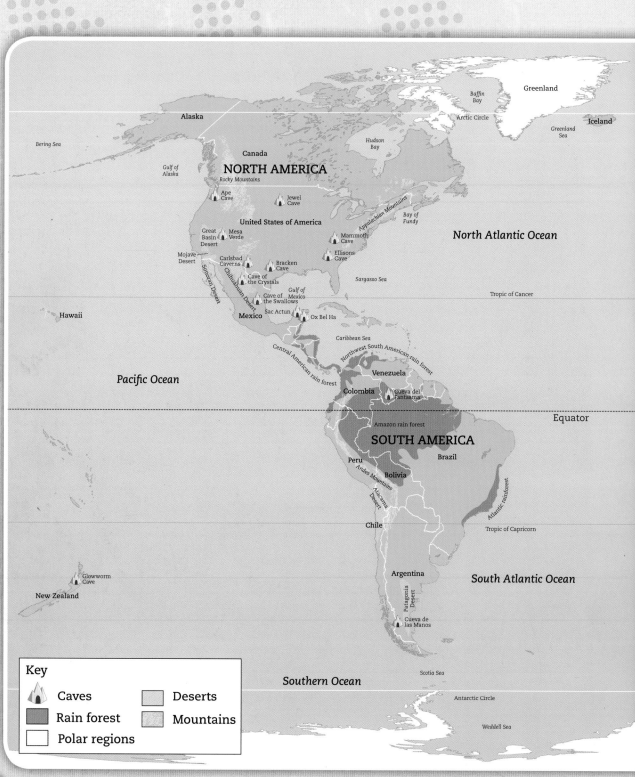

Greenland

Baffin
Bay

Arctic Circle

Iceland

Alaska

Greenland
Sea

Bering Sea

Hudson
Bay

Gulf of
Alaska

Canada

NORTH AMERICA

Rocky Mountains

Ape
Cave

Jewel
Cave

Appalachian Mountains

Bay of
Fundy

North Atlantic Ocean

United States of America

Great
Basin
Desert

Mesa
Verde

Mammoth
Cave

Mojave
Desert

Carlsbad
Caverns

Bracken
Cave

Ellisons
Cave

Sonoran Desert

Chihuahuan Desert

Cave of
the Crystals

Sargasso Sea

Tropic of Cancer

Hawaii

Cave of
the Swallows

Gulf of
Mexico

Mexico

Sac Actun

Ox Bel Ha

Caribbean Sea

Central American rain forest

Northwest South American rain forest

Pacific Ocean

Venezuela

Colombia

Cueva del
Fantasma

Amazon rain forest

Equator

SOUTH AMERICA

Peru

Brazil

Bolivia

Andes Mountains

Atacama
Desert

Atlantic rainforest

Chile

Tropic of Capricorn

Glowworm
Cave

Argentina

South Atlantic Ocean

New Zealand

Patagonia
Desert

Cueva de
las Manos

Scotia Sea

Southern Ocean

Antarctic Circle

Weddell Sea

Key

Caves

Deserts

Rain forest

Mountains

Polar regions

This map shows you where to find some of the world's caves. There are many other exciting places to discover. Why not explore the oceans, rain forests, deserts, and mountains shown on the map?

Arctic Ocean

Kara Sea

Laptev Sea

East Siberian Sea

Barents Sea

Norwegian Sea

Sweden

Finland

Norway

Russia

Arctic Circle

Bering Sea

Fingal's Cave

North Sea

Sea of Okhotsk

United Kingdom

Gaping Gill

Dan-yr-Ogof

EUROPE

Eisriesenwelt

Postojna Cave

Krubera-Voronja

France

Austria

Bay of Biscay

Chauvet Cave

Alps

Slovenia

Black Sea

Caucasus Mountains

Georgia

Lascaux Caves

Raymonden Shelter

Caspian Sea

Kara Kum Desert

Takla Makan Desert

Gobi Desert

Sea of Japan

Japan

Azykh Cave

Karakoram Range

ASIA

Yellow Sea

Atlas Mountains

Mediterranean Sea

Himalayas

China

Pacific Ocean

Sahara Desert

Red Sea

Arabian Desert

Thar Desert

Bhimbetka

East China Sea

India

AFRICA

Arabian Sea

Bay of Bengal

Southeast Asian rain forest

South China Sea

Sulu Sea

Malaysia

Sarawak Chamber

Central African rain forest

Indonesian rain forest

Banda Sea

Indonesia

Indian Ocean

AUSTRALIA

Mozambique Channel

Madagascar

Madagascan rain forest

Coral Sea

Namib Desert

Botswana

Great Sandy Desert

Australia

Northern Australian rain forest

Kalahari Desert

Simpson Desert

Gibson Desert

South Africa

Drakensberg Mountains

Great Victoria Desert

Great Dividing Range

Tasman Sea

Blombos Cave

N

Southern Ocean

Antarctic Circle

ANTARCTICA

Mount Erebus

Ross Sea

TIMELINE

c. 1 million years ago	Azykh Cave in Azerbaijan is occupied by early humans
c. 300,000 years ago	Early Neanderthals live in Azykh Cave
c. 80,000 years ago	Early humans create art in Blombos Cave, in South Africa
c. 20,000 years ago	San people create cave paintings in Drakensberg, South Africa
c. 20,000 years ago	The stone-age cave art of Lascaux is painted
c. 10,000 years ago	Hand paintings are created at Cueva de las Manos
c. 450 BCE	Greek playwright Euripides uses a cave as his writing place
1772 CE	Joseph Banks visits and names Fingal's Cave
1797	Mammoth Cave in Kentucky is first discovered
1838	Stephen Bishop begins exploring and mapping Mammoth Cave
1880s	Edouard Martel begins his pioneering cave explorations
1888	An ancient human skeleton is discovered in Raymonden Shelter, France
1890s	Jovan Cvijić publishes his important work on karst landscapes
1920s	Norbert Casteret pioneers the sport of cave diving
1940	The Lascaux cave paintings are discovered
1942	Scuba gear is invented, making cave diving much easier
1958	Mathematician Leland W. Sprinkle completes the Stalacpipe Organ
1981	Sarawak Chamber, the world's biggest underground chamber, is discovered on Borneo
2000	The Cave of the Crystals is discovered in Mexico

FACT FILE

CAVE RECORDS

Longest cave system: Mammoth Cave, Kentucky, USA	390 miles (628 kilometers)
Longest underwater cave system: Ox Bel Ha, Mexico	144 miles (230 kilometers)
Deepest cave: Krubera-Voronja Cave, Georgia	7,189 feet (2,191 meters) deep
Biggest bat colony: Bracken Cave, Texas, USA	20 million

CAVE STUDIES

Speleology	The study of caves
Biospeleology	The study of cave life
Speleopaleontology	The study of fossils found in caves
Speleoarchaeologists	The study of human artifacts found in caves
Hydrogeology	The study of underground water
Karst geomorphology	The study of the formation of caves and other karst landforms

TYPES OF CAVE-DWELLERS

Trogloxenes	Creatures that visit caves
Troglophiles	Creatures that prefer to live in caves
Troglobites	Creatures that live only in caves
Troglodytes	Human cave dwellers

SPELEOTHEM GUIDE

Stalactite	Rock formation that grows downward from the ceiling
Stalagmite	Rock formation that builds upward from the floor
Pillar/column	Floor-to-ceiling formation made when a stalactite and a stalagmite meet
Flowstone	Smooth speleothem that coats a wall or surface
Rimstone dam	Wall that builds up around water
Soda straw	Thin, tube-shaped stalactite
Helictite	Spiraling stalactite
Drip curtain	Thin, folded sheet
Snottite	Looks like a stalactite, but is made of bacteria covered in slime

GLOSSARY

abseil move down a vertical surface, such as the side of a cave, by using a rope

bacterium (plural: **bacteria**) type of tiny, single-celled living thing

cave diving exploring underwater caves

crampons spikes that fit onto shoes or boots to add grip on ice and snow

dolomite type of rock that can be dissolved to form caves

drip curtain speleothem shaped like a thin draped or folded sheet

fieldwork scientific study in a cave or elsewhere outside the laboratory

flowstone smooth speleothem (rock formation) formed by cave water running across a surface

glacier large flow of ice moving slowly downhill

glacier cave hollow cave formed inside a glacier

gypsum type of rock that can be dissolved to form caves

hypothermia dangerous illness caused by a person's body temperature falling too low

ice cave rock cave with ice formations inside

karst type of landscape made up of rocks that can be dissolved to form caves

laboratory workroom with equipment for doing scientific study or experiments

limestone type of rock that can be dissolved to form caves

marble type of rock that can be dissolved to form caves

microorganism microscopically small living thing

Neanderthal species of early human that has now died out

ocher type of naturally yellow or reddish earth or clay

rimstone dam speleothem that forms a low wall around pools of water

scuba underwater breathing equipment (stands for "Self-Contained Underwater Breathing Apparatus")

snottite hanging tube of slime containing cave bacteria

species particular type of living thing

speleology study of caves

speleothem rock formation found inside a cave

stalactite speleothem (rock formation) that grows downward from the ceiling

stalagmite speleothem (rock formation) that builds upward from the floor

troglobite living thing found only inside caves

troglophile living thing that prefers to live in caves

trogloxene living thing that spends some of its time in caves and some outside

FIND OUT MORE

Books

Carson, Mary Kay. *The Bat Scientists* (Scientists in the Field). Boston: Houghton Mifflin, 2010.

Champion, Neil. *Wild Underground: Caves and Caving* (Adventure Outdoors). Mankato, Minn.: Smart Apple Media, 2013.

Miller, Sara Swan. *Secret Lives of Cave Creatures* (Secret Lives). New York: Marshall Cavendish Benchmark, 2010.

Mills, J. Elizabeth. *The Creation of Caves* (Land Formation). New York: Rosen, 2010.

Rosenberg, Pam. *Cave Crawlers* (Landform Adventures). Chicago: Raintree, 2012.

Web sites

www.caverntours.com/KIDSPAGE_Home.html
This fun activity site includes cave facts, puzzles, and more.

www.lascaux.culture.fr/#/en/02_00.xml
Try out the amazing 3D virtual tour that lets you explore Lascaux's famous cave paintings.

www.teachersdomain.org/resource/ess05.sci.ess.earthsys.virtmap
This site has a clickable cave system with many photos.

DVDs

Cave of Forgotten Dreams (directed by Werner Herzog, 2010)
This 3D film is about the cave paintings in Chauvet Cave in France.

Planet Earth (directed by Alastair Fothergill, 2006)
Episode 4 of this TV series explores caves and their incredible wildlife.

Places to visit

Mammoth Cave

Mammoth Cave National Park, 1 Mammoth Cave Parkway
Mammoth Cave, Kentucky 42259
www.nps.gov/maca/index.htm

Glowworm Cave

Waitomo Caves Road, Otorohanga, New Zealand
www.waitomo.com/waitomo-glowworm-caves.aspx

Jenolan Caves

Jenolan Caves Road, Hartley, NSW, Australia
www.jenolancaves.org.au

Further research

Which part of this book was the most interesting to you? You could
try finding out more about one of the cave-inspired topics below or
whatever you enjoyed reading about the most:

- Search for pictures of troglobites (cave creatures that only live in
  caves). What features do they all share? Cave plants and animals
  are often rare and endangered, as they are only found in particular
  caves. See if you can find out about some endangered cave species.

- If you like the cave paintings in this book, try searching for more
  cave art online or in your local library. Use it to inspire your own
  cave art creations. What materials and tools could you use to make
  it look as realistic as possible?

- Professor Penny Boston searches for caves on other planets, where
  living things might one day be discovered. Do you think we will
  find alien life one day? What would it be like? See if you can find
  out more about how scientists are testing for life on other planets.
  You could start with planetary probes, Mars meteorites, and SETI
  (the Search for Extra-Terrestrial Intelligence).

INDEX